Dim Sum

Dim Sum

A Pocket Guide

by Kit Shan Li

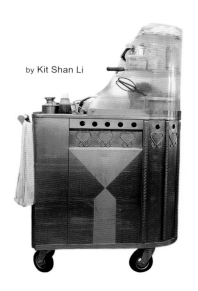

CHRONICLE BOOKS
SAN FRANCISCO

Library of Congress Cataloging-in-Publication Data available.

ISBN 0-8118-4178-2

Manufactured in China

Photography Consultation by Sunny Sung

Distributed in Canada by Raincoast Books
9050 Shaughnessy Street
Vancouver, British Columbia V6P 6E5

10 9 8 7 6 5 4 3 2 1

Chronicle Books LLC
85 Second Street
San Francisco, California 94105

www.chroniclebooks.com

An Important Note from the Author

Dim Sum is a reference book based on my experience; the dim sum descriptions detail what I found to be the most typical preparations. Dishes by the same name may differ from restaurant to restaurant. If you are a vegetarian or have food allergies, please consult the servers or the restaurant manager before you order. Relax and enjoy a good meal. Thank you!

MENU
菜單

INTRODUCTION 簡介

About this Book

The purpose of this book is to help non-Chinese speakers order Chinese dim sum. It may also be useful to Chinese speakers in the restaurant industry who may have difficulty understanding and communicating with their English-speaking customers.

It is always enjoyable for me to try food from different cultures. For the same reason, I hope this little manual will clear up some of the mysteries and uncertainties that can make dim sum seem intimidating or simply strange, and it will help create an opportunity for people of all cultures to enjoy this delicious—and fun—dining experience. Let's eat and share together!

How to Use this Book

This book is organized in five chapters, each representing a category of dim sum: steamed, deep-fried, pan-fried, congee, and dessert. A photograph is provided for every item, all taken at Chinese restaurants I visited in the United States and Hong Kong, to help you recognize the various dim sum passing on the carts.

Alongside each photo, you'll find the name of the item in traditional Chinese characters, the Cantonese pronunciation, the English name of the dim sum, and a brief description. The Cantonese pronunciation is given in the form of transliteration. The objective is to enable an English speaker with no linguistic training to produce an approximate pronunciation that, given the proper context, should be fairly intelligible to the Cantonese listener.

Walk in for Dim Sum

Cantonese people like to go to restaurants in the morning and have dim sum for breakfast or brunch; for some, it's a daily ritual. These dim sum establishments are generally very casual, and large groups of families and friends often gather together there for a weekend brunch. Now dim sum enthusiasts in the United States and elsewhere have made it a popular choice for lunch, too. Most restaurants that serve dim sum welcome guests without reservations. When you walk into the restaurant, often the first thing you are asked is, "How many people?" To enter into the spirit of a meeting of cultures encouraged by this book, you could answer as follows:

English	Chinese Character	Cantonese Pronunciation
1 Person	一位	yut why
2 People	兩位	long why
3 People	三位	sahm why
4 People	四位	say why
5 People	五位	mm why
6 People	六位	look why
7 People	七位	chut why
8 People	八位	baht why
9 People	九位	gao why
10 People	十位	sup why
11 People	十一位	sup yut why
12 People	十二位	sup yee why

Tea

Once seated, the next thing you will likely be asked is, "What kind of tea would you like?" Tea is a traditional complement for dim sum and a very important part of the dining ritual. To ask for a new pot of tea, say "yut woo _____" (fill in the blank with your tea of choice; see list below).

Here are some of the common choices:

English	Chinese Character	Cantonese Pronunciation
Oolong Tea	烏龍茶	woo long cha
Jasmine Tea	香片茶	hong peen cha
Poo Nei Tea	普洱茶	po lay cha
Daffodil Tea	水仙茶	suey seen cha
Iron Buddha Tea	鐵觀音茶	tit gwoon yum cha

To indicate to the waiter or waitress that you're ready for a refill of your teapot, simply lift the lid of the teapot like this:

The waiter gives each table a record card like this for dim sum ordering:

檯號		人數						
小點								
中點								
大點								
特點								
頂點								
廚點								
飲品								
廚食								

Small → 小點
Medium → 中點
Large → 大點
Extra-Large → 特點
Extra-Extra-Large → 頂點

侍應		TOTAL	
		TAX	
		GRAND TOTAL	

Ordering

Once seated and with your steaming tea in hand, you can observe one of the most unique aspects of having dim sum: ordering it. Servers push around carts laden with various dim sum items, circling the restaurant like a parade. Customers select as many items as they like from passing carts. As you choose dishes, your server will stamp or mark the record card supplied at the outset of the meal. The record card is divided into sections where a tally of items is made by price category. These categories vary from restaurant to restaurant, but most often include small, medium, large, extra-large, and extra-extra-large. As you would guess, small is the cheapest, with the price generally increasing with the size of the item. The price category doesn't always correspond to the physical size of the dish, however; some small delicacies may have a comparatively big price, and vice versa.

To ask for the check, signal to the serving person and say, "my dahn." Your waiter will calculate the bill by counting the stamps or marks on your record card.

Condiments

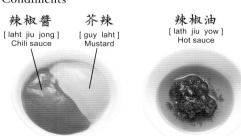

辣椒醬
[laht jiu jong]
Chili sauce

芥辣
[guy laht]
Mustard

辣椒油
[lath jiu yow]
Hot sauce

Legend — Thank the Chinese Emperor

One day, the emperor Qian Long of China and his subordinates visited Jiang Nan. The emperor didn't want the townspeople to recognize him, so he was dressed casually, in the clothes of a commoner. Desiring a rest and some refreshment, the emperor and his fellows stopped by a tea house. A waiter came and set several bowls on their table. Then he held a kettle high in the air and poured tea into one of the bowls. The tea flowed into the bowl like water falls from a cliff to the ground, and not even one drop was spilled. The emperor was amazed. He then took up the kettle and imitated the waiter, pouring tea from a height into the rest of the bowls. Watching their emperor pour tea for them, his fellows wanted to kneel and kowtow to the emperor in the traditional manner of respect. They could not, as they were afraid the gesture would reveal the emperor's identity. Instead, one of the subordinates curled his fingers and knocked on the table to symbolize the kneel-and-kowtow gesture. As this legend tells it, that is why Chinese people knock on the table to indicate gratitude or to say thank you when other people pour tea for them.

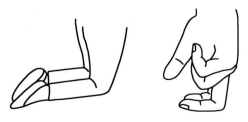

How to Use Chopsticks

Chinese people use chopsticks for eating all the time, the way Americans use a fork and knife. Learning to use chopsticks can be a little difficult in the beginning, but don't give up; once you master the skill, it's easy, and eating with chopsticks can add to the appreciation of foods from countries where chopsticks are used. Follow the five steps below and practice first by picking up light objects such as cotton balls.

1 Hold your dominant hand as if you are going to shake hands with someone.

2 Secure the first chopstick in the crook between your thumb and index finger.

3 Place the second chopstick on top and hold it with your thumb and index finger.

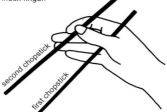

4 Tuck your ring finger underneath the first (lower) chopstick.

5 Tuck your middle finger underneath the second (upper) chopstick. To pick up food, move the second chopstick up and down to grip pieces with the ends of the two chopsticks.

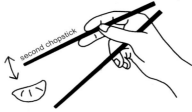

Glossary of Unusual Ingredients

Chinese hair vegetable

Chinese hair vegetable grows in China in plateaus high above sea level. It is so named because it does indeed look like hair. It is almost flavorless, with a texture similar to seaweed.

Sweet lotus-seed paste

Thick, sweet lotus-seed paste is made from lotus seed, groundnut oil, and sugar syrup. It has a nutty flavor.

Preserved pork belly

This pork product is cured by air-drying. It is similar to bacon, but it has a stronger flavor.

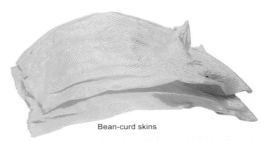

Bean-curd skins

Made from dried soy milk, these skins are flavorless but pleasant in texture. They are used to wrap fillings or as a bed for serving some dishes.

Taro

Edible root with a high starch content and a taste similar to potatoes, taro plays a similar role, adding earthy flavor and body to a variety of dishes.

Preserved Chinese sausage

This air-dried pork sausage has
a taste that is both salty and sweet.

Chinese dried mushrooms

Often used in Chinese dishes, dried mushrooms
have a richer and more intense flavor than fresh
shiitake mushrooms.

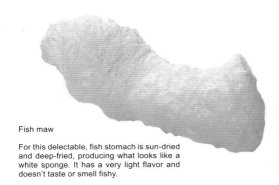

Fish maw

For this delectable, fish stomach is sun-dried and deep-fried, producing what looks like a white sponge. It has a very light flavor and doesn't taste or smell fishy.

Water chestnuts

Water chestnuts are corms, not nuts. After the dark skin is peeled, the flesh should be white in color. Water chestnuts are sweet and are eaten either raw or cooked.

Chapter 1

蒸

Steamed

蝦餃
[ha gow]

Shrimp Dumpling

wrapping: tang-flour dough
filling: shrimp, bamboo shoots

Shrimp dumplings are considered the most popular dim sum.
If you like shrimp, I highly recommend this one!

燒賣
[siu my]

Pork Dumpling

wrapping: plain flour and egg dough
filling: pork, shrimp

Don't swallow the bones.

鳳爪

[foong jow]

Chicken Feet

The look of these marinated chicken feet may be off-putting to some, but they actually taste yummy! This is my Japanese friend's favorite—he won't share it with other people!

山竹牛肉
[sahn jook (ng)ow yook]

Beef Ball

ground beef balls served on top of bean-curd skins

雞扎
[guy jaht]

Chicken Meat Roll

wrapping: bean-curd skin
filling: chicken, taro, fish maw, ham,
Chinese dried mushrooms

鴨腳札

[(ng)ahp geuk jaht]

Duck Feet Roll

wrapping: bean-curd skin
filling: duck feet, taro

牛柏葉

[(ng)ow pahk yeep]

Beef Tripe

marinated beef tripe, usually cooked with
shredded green or red bell peppers

排骨
[pie gwat]

Spareribs

spareribs, usually seasoned with
black beans and red chili peppers

糯米雞
[nor my guy]

Glutinous Rice with Chicken

wrapping: lotus leaf (not edible)
filling: glutinous rice, chicken, Chinese dried mushrooms,
dried shrimp, pork

潮州粉果

[chiu jow fun gwat]

Chao Zhou Dumpling

wrapping: tang-flour dough
filling: pork, bamboo shoots, peanuts, dried shrimp

鯪魚球
[lang yü kow]

Fish Ball

ground fish, usually mixed with a dash of finely
chopped dried orange peel and Chinese hair vegetable

魷魚

[yow yü]

Squid

squid marinated in a shrimp paste

Served with a ginger and
vinegar dipping sauce.

灌湯餃
[goon tong gow]

Giant Dumpling

wrapping: plain flour and egg dough
filling: usually pork, shrimp, scallops,
Chinese dried mushrooms

魚翅餃
[yü chee gow]

"Shark Fin" Dumpling

wrapping: plain flour and egg dough
filling: pork, dried shrimp, bamboo shoots,
Chinese dried mushrooms

These dumplings are shaped with a ridge on top that looks like
a shark's fin, but do not actually contain shark meat.

鮮竹卷

[seen jook goon]

Bean Curd Roll

wrapping: bean-curd skin
filling: pork, bamboo shoots, shrimp

牛肚

[(ng)ow toe]

Beef Stomach

beef stomach marinated in ground black pepper

Served with sweet soy sauce.

蝦腸粉
[ha chong fun]

Shrimp Rice Roll

wrapping: ground rice, water
filling: shrimp

Served with sweet soy sauce.

牛肉腸粉

[(ng)ow yook chong fun]

Beef Rice Roll

wrapping: ground rice, water
filling: seasoned ground beef

41

Served with sweet soy sauce.

叉燒腸粉
[cha siu chong fun]

Barbecued Pork Rice Roll

wrapping: ground rice, water
filling: barbecued pork

馬拉糕
[ma lie go]
Brown Sugar Sponge Cake

plain flour, butter, eggs, brown sugar, evaporated milk

Although this cake is sweet and soft, it is not a dessert dish.

奶黃飽
[nye wong bao]

Egg Custard Bun

Peel the paper
before you eat.

wrapping: plain flour dough
filling: sweet egg custard

蓮蓉飽
[leen yoong bao]

Lotus-Seed Paste Bun

Peel the paper
before you eat.

wrapping: plain flour dough
filling: sweet lotus-seed paste

叉燒飽
[cha siu bao]

Barbecued Pork Bun

Peel the paper
before you eat.

wrapping: plain flour dough
filling: barbecued pork

46

雞 飽
[guy bao]

Chicken Bun

Peel the paper before you eat.

wrapping: plain flour dough
filling: chicken, Chinese dried mushrooms, Chinese cabbage

Chapter 2

Deep-fried

春卷
[chun goon]

Spring Roll

wrapping: plain wheat flour dough
filling: pork, mushrooms, bamboo shoots

煎堆
[jean dway]

Sesame Ball

wrapping: glutinous rice flour covered with sesame seeds
filling: sweet lotus-seed paste

炸雲吞
[jar won ton]

Deep-Fried Wonton

wrapping: wonton skin
filling: pork, shrimp

炸魷魚鬚

[jar yow yü so]

Deep-Fried Squid Tentacles

People who like Italian fried calamari
would enjoy this crispy and chewy dish.

咸 水 角
[hahm suey gock]
Meat-Filled Ball

wrapping: glutinous rice flour
filling: pork, vegetables

芋 角

[woo gock]

Taro Ball

wrapping: mashed taro
filling: pork, dried shrimp

Chapter 3

煎

Pan-fried

蘿蔔糕
[law bahk go]

White Turnip Cake

turnip, rice flour, preserved Chinese sausage, dried shrimp,
preserved pork belly, Chinese dried mushrooms

芋頭糕
[woo tao go]

Taro Cake

taro, rice flour, preserved Chinese sausage,
preserved pork belly, dried shrimp

馬蹄糕
[ma tie go]

Water-Chestnut Cake

water chestnuts, water-chestnut flour

Stuffed Eggplant

煎釀青椒

[jean yong chang jiu]

Stuffed Peppers

green bell peppers stuffed with ground fish

Some Chinese restaurants may have
stuffed eggplant as well.

煎韭菜餅
[jean gow choy bang]

Chive Dumplings

wrapping: tang flour
filling: chives, shrimp

煎蝦米腸粉
[jean ha my chong fun]

Dried Shrimp Rice Rolls

rice roll made with a mixture of ground rice,
water, dried shrimp, and scallions

Usually served with hoisin sauce and sesame paste.

Chapter 4

粥

Congee

Congee is a souplike dish made with rice. A variety
of different vegetables and meats can be added to
create different flavors. Congee is typically eaten for
breakfast in China.

皮蛋瘦肉粥
[pay dahn sow yook jook]

Preserved Duck Egg Congee

congee with preserved duck eggs and pork

preserved
duck egg

66

艇仔粥
[tang jai jook]

Boat Congee

congee with squid, peanuts, pigskin, and
ground beef with fried rice noodles

squid

ground beef
mixed with
fried noodles

pigskin

peanut

67

碎牛粥

[suey (ng)ow jook]

Ground Beef Congee

congee with ground beef
and fried rice noodles

ground beef
mixed with
fried noodles

魚片粥

[yü peen jook]

Fish Congee

congee with sliced fish

sliced fish

柴魚花生粥
[chai yü fa sung jook]

Dried Fish Peanut Congee

congee with dried fish and peanuts

peanut

dried fish

豬 紅 粥

[jü hoong jook]

Pig's Blood Congee

congee with cubes of pig's blood

The texture of prepared pig's blood
is similar to a firm tofu, and is very tasty.

pig's blood

Chapter 5

甜品

Dessert

芝麻卷
[jee ma goon]

Black Sesame Roll

If you like the white sesame seeds familiar to loaves of bread,
bagels, and other baked goods, try the black sesame roll.
The black seeds produce a stronger flavor than white
and are pleasantly aromatic.

椰汁糕
[yeh jup go]

Coconut Milk Gelatin

coconut milk, sugar, egg white, and gelatin

The texture of this delicate dessert is similar to a soufflé.
It has a sweet coconut taste.

芝麻糊
[jee ma woo]

Black Sesame Soup

sweet liquid dessert made with finely ground black sesame

蛋撻

[dahn taht]

Egg Custard Tart

crust: flour and egg dough
filling: sweet egg custard

brown sugar

豆腐花
[dao fu fa]

Tofu Pudding

Tofu pudding is just like the soft,
creamy version of tofu called silken tofu.
Served hot or cold with brown sugar or syrup.

芒果布甸
[mong gwor bo deen]

Mango Pudding

sweet mango, gelatin, and egg

ACKNOWLEDGMENTS 鳴謝

Sincere thanks to Steve Heller for introducing me to Chronicle Books, and deep thanks to Chronicle for giving me a precious opportunity to introduce this tasty aspect of Chinese culture to others.

To my family, 爸爸、媽媽、姐姐、哥哥, thank you for going out to have dim sum with me every day, especially my mom, who accompanied me the most. Thanks to my sister for paying all the bills! Sincere thanks to Sunny Sung, for helping me with the beautiful images. A big thanks to Frank Martinez, who provided me with excellent advice. Renqiu Yu, thank you for helping me proofread the content. Great thanks to Hui Kwan Ming for his twenty-four-hour emergency support! Special thanks to all my other friends and classmates, who pitched in and contributed to the progress of this book. And lastly, thank you to all the readers who are interested in Chinese culture. Enjoy!